SKULL-FILLED SUN

Is A Rose Press

2018

SKULL-FILLED SUN

poems

Valérie Déus

Poetry

Cover artwork: *Erzulie Inanna* by Joy Spika
Cover and book design: Jacob Palm

ISBN   978-0-9896245-3-4

Is a Rose Press publishes poetry, experimental writing, hybrid and other work. We are a cooperative editorial board of writers in the virtual world. Submissions are by invitation only at this time. Check our website for updates and changes in this policy.

Website: isarosepress.WordPress.com

is a rose press
minneapolis-missoula

To my family
and
To Haiti via New York

Spark 2016

We're going to run
all over this city tonight

every one way
every full stop

brown girls in skirts
create the black light

while the helix haired
barter in hugs

drum dreamers thrive
in the afterglow

while shadows
interrupt the grain

eating cheese curds
how bout you?

There's a funnel cake
in my future puzzle

hippies still preaching love
even with the weather report
crawling all over this ultraviolet night

A man declares
his soul surrenders to the dark side
and I believe him
I mean, he's nothing to
his puppet leaders

bugs attracted to the brights
sticking to the glass

others hang back in the black
See? We all hate standing in the light

with a breeze coming in from the west
that last kiss wasn't intentional

It's my knees
I lose them to smiles on bikes
with locs illuminated by the dawn

Bar Hopping

Farm

Under a coil oven sky
I cross the street
with a head full of ink

and I pocket the beginnings
of a garden plot
and a woman in yellow

watches me and
I try to remember
if I know her from school
work or the other bits of my life

the sky is cloudy but no
there won't be rain yet

I buy tights at Capezio from Tina
her husband calls while I hand her my money

9am and the keys
to my socialization
is Papi's Taxi
the Upper East Side
and climbing the hill there

I wear a tie
on my first day
I fake tough into realness
the shell to protect
my inner tomato

Natalie had her period
and her orange mouth
like of a cave in St. Marc
told us where babies came from

Denise's lunch comes by limo
never late at half past 12

her mother said vodou came from Haiti
and not Africa so we couldn't be the same

Dion

at Issac Hayes's Birthday party
I declare my love to Dionne Warwick

I gush about her purring eyes
and lethal side smile

how her voice brings me
to Solid Gold dancers
Marilyn McCoo, skinned knees
my Nana learning English from Video Music Box

I explain how her piercing cheek bones
are the same mountains on the faces
on my mother's side of the family
the mountains in Haiti

I whisper to her my dream
of her and Stephanie Mills
singing a duet that aligns
the planets

she turns to me and sighs "Thank yuh baby"
followed by a smile releasing a stream cigarette smoke into
my face.

Come-ons

I sit right there   at the bar
sip my drink   and wait
for you   to meet me
then to   the movies

where   we will
lengthen   ourselves
and buckle under   the weight
of corn and brown sugar water
with Pe Demeran as chaperon

we walk   and talk
about the smallest part of our days
yours filled with customers
who won't consume   bruised frozen corn
or the tomatoes you touched

the milk   goes badly
in their kitchens and   chickens won't
egg for cheap thrill

mine on   the E train
where men   dangle their principles
on girls in uniforms
some smoke comma
splices wiping fragments
all over the seat
peppering the car
with run-ons come-ons.

Miscarried

In the third
month of letters
the waves were not perfect
their distrustful tossing
boils away the salt
spreading into the city like floodwaters

as an exchange you reach outward
with the whole of your body
chin forward and a blunder of breast
embracing life's private wars
like tangled bundles on brown shoulders

we hang fog from the street lights
outside our window
the elevated train is a ghost today
rain-wet fast screams
it cut through dimness
and thoughtless haunts
during the prelude
you ask where we were going

we read the lines
and did what they told us
the limbo of what was
said and unsaid
the present longs for closure
seen and unseen
yet there isn't anything
but the road of what's left to write

the homes smile on dead end streets
and under worn rooftops
their tabletops lay
in pale silence
like a breath
drawn in and held

for fear
of being left behind
for fear
of being forgotten
but we never questioned where we were

would it be possible to discuss this with you?
they say a face stains an ordinary life
a life that leaves soup
to cool on the counter

and laundry to pile
while there is much of you to spend
in your round mouth
the face is paved in stones

the time between us won't last
in an instant the steel river exposes its bones
and spits them forth
I watch as I breathe in
the promise of something undelivered

Told

I tell something
told

I remember blue
I let time pass

And I am now both
simple and much

It's called blame
but blue is so
that it gets hair and under the skin

I suppose
I bring blame
back from the faithful beloved

I dead travel
by the all blush-of-the-world
not dangerous
but an unknown red

I tell and see sorry
from a position of hope
and not of blame

but to plead and to let one
be visible to twisting

the time is long but
whatever happens
the call will be soon
after I find home

We, Delancey

together
driving across
the Williamsburg Bridge
keeps us close
away from
talking when crossing Canal

looking for cure root
applied twice a week
to the affected areas
by the upper east shoulder
downtown past Duane street shins

sliced the day
because we shaved and showered
because your lover
loves movies
because my head is your souvenir

in other news
there's no change
at the corner of 70th and Madison
just little pleated skirts
and gray blazers complaints
about the limitations of rainbows

they wonder out loud
why we are here

We could split ourselves
into 18 ways of waiting at JFK

and not be home for hours
until we go from high to elevated
until your mother has
all the women in white pray for us
and end Mondays once and for all

Ocean Avenue

are you my lonely

poem
dancing? will the line break

in a fit of rage

rearranging pictures
according to sly and sex
in low light
intention almost slip away

an unfamiliar memory
hidden below your 24-hour edge of caffeine

when you name the work a body
a curious life emerges

from blade of moon
a net of risk and promise
this empty space is not
empty when one isn't afraid

it is a placeholder these premonitions of home
and it's all tied up in the definition of being.

Dekalb

I loved you
according to the laws
of distance in the un-lived
space between friends
the way saying   "just between friends"
disarms the full day

the way Lew's "anything goes" attitude
and his soft severity like a TV dad
makes him the perfect summer peach
with a side of buttered brown bread

the way we were ruined before it rained
you run the water like it's free
and marinate in salt and lavender
the light bulb stews overhead

the way you say somewhere we
were real lovers in some old borrowed life
where the tip of my nose
hides in the tender of your neck

a life where we breathe
sleep and be our everyday slipper selves

Ditmas

Living in this fever
talking like it's new

like heat is a modern invention
and never seen before this moment
instead of a homecoming

blood and bones
speak Easter Sunday hot comb

these lungs
hug in my ribcage
wet newspaper breath
and gag again and again

outside bodies on the asphalt
take the road by foot
but beneath the bodies are more bodies

what does it
look like when
just breathing risks drowning
just sitting remembers sinking
just movement recalls swimming
living in submerged

Bridges

In and out

out and done
you bring out the 2nd box of tissues
this week, it's almost lunch
and you move quickly past the robots handing out
lottery tickets in the back of the room
you rub lwil maskriti on masterful jabs
death by millions of gleaming teeth
is worse than the quick death blow
tag out of the ring
on the 2:30 train
to anywhere but this daily mortal combat

These Miles

These miles are mine
thick and lush
I keep them with me
tucked between la vierge prayer cards

so walk your ass home with your guitar
Mr. Brown, your fingernails are calling you

to turn a day into smoke
into alleluia howl
stop the day from becoming plain ol' panties

we yawn instead busy blushing
too bloody and holy
still sipping on yesterday's yesterday

be the perfect family flirt
while practicing being human
while we pour past Robyn's Vintage 1st ave dream.

Hot Bite

In my blackest dream
we kick the day
out of a city sky
and write you back to life over and over

In my blackest dream
we sip Malta's hushed loops
spilling black song from our lips
and talk of being dangerous

In my blackest dream
we are a ritual away
from being a hurricane

In my blackest dream
we haven't got time for the pain
but the itch in my palms says we'll find a way

The Streets of Brooklyn

feed off various languages

ki moun -
copper legs seek roots
we orbit unseen religions
visible only to the initiated
unknowable from the line in the middle of the road

still sacred even in the rain
you are ti mafi
you are ti madam
wearing mama's hair under a headscarf

we move underground
day workers and night laborers
fuel a 24- hour subway running

kote-
face the skull filled sun and
straighten our godmother's zanno
these people don't know us
they don't know we don't care what they think

beyond the rings of Flatbush
to the 3rd moon of Haiti
we reinvent our lives
by swallowing the night

a seat by the window
to skin yucca and greetings
mayor neighbors on the periphery
with Nana's blood sewn into the curb

ki jan-

we rename you
use it covertly
you etranje a stranger
something between
nightmare and applause

we weave our tongues
around recipes
ingredients and spice talk
exchange compliments

Bridge Uprising

we walk side by side
blue and red across the bridge
blood proud wave towards the plaza

in this reunion
we feed the canyon our rage
sliding off downtown glass and
sun soaked towers

our time spilled black
into a hushed loop of sound
we bring bruises and signs

we crowd this steel ribcage
like rice with extra beans
the clean grid beams delicate with shadows
before spilling heavy into the early morning

Knowing

I was gonna tag you but got Saturday-morning distracted.
Magic 8 ball sees cosplay in my future
and serves me a side of daydreams.

I take Queens size minutes to our doppelgänger's house
near the curb to catch up with our undead who wore sweat
like lace.

at Soon Deli, I grab popcorn for the salt
and you hit the hot foods,
Spanish rice, chicken flats and avocados

Every day, I risk my heart
but get stuck on getting A's.
It's hard to be real with the devil you know.

on the pier with this heartache in my lap,
I lick grease from your warm mouth
a masterpiece at 2 am.

what else are 2 people supposed to do
on a Saturday night in an American city?
We can only bleed who we are.

Misdirection

this place is strange and I am strange in it
this air
catches at my nape
I notice, it's darker
than I remember September to be
the way freeze
commits its self to my frame
earlier and earlier
helps me forget
I ever had a face
a version of me bobbing away above my shoulders
a black gesture looking for the sea

tomorrow, everyone will go home
to their strangest dreams
we'll take the lead and remake ourselves
into more than neon lakes

the night slicks our hair
and I think this is like sex
tender and rolling towards misdirection
a soft dark landscape
the last place to be when wanting this much

After Skulls

We walk and walk
tender friend
we bob and weave
on a shadow of sleep
With slogans and signs
With coffee and cola
With checkered bags with this morning's rice beans
and last night's red sauce chicken

our magic keeps
us afloat
soft bubbles of hair
With flags and blankets
and the drumming
and the drumming

we hold hands
bob and walk
on routes
of asphalt
we sing
your grace
surfaces and is lifted
by waves of drumming

Amber Resin

Tati curls her hair
and saves it for the ride
under an indigo blue scarf
she is all amber resin and cloves
and I'm convinced that this is what gods smell like

our way to the airport
is lined with kompas on heavy rotation
drum solos leading into robust horns
tell me when trying to fall out of love
don't sit under a smart well-fed moon
it can only curve you into your own belly
you'll need patience to tight walk between
feeling and feeling too much
sometime tea helps

Tati laughs at the wheel between tears
tapping on her brown skin cigarettes

love is a tablet pistach
this hard-sweet bite is matched
by small sigh kisses
submerged in sucked teeth

nan domi

with bien etre night sweats
I drip fragrant in the street
over freshly minted rats and under water towers dogs
I batter and bigged my hair nan domi
In sleep how did I get this far in the cold

winks dividing the sorry from the stable
what happens nan domi doesn't always stay there
sometime sleep stalks the whole morning
staying with me way between van stops
soaking me in sheets and visions

neighbors discuss their dreams like news
starting with "Last night, I had the strangest dream...
while riding up and down the escalators
what we do nan domi lives
between neighbors and seat cushions
between the sheets and our metal parts
between us and our gods

I am best when I dream of flying
not on my fucking feet
selling popcorn for the salt or cigarettes for the shakes
not killing all my familiar faces and removing my bones
one by one

Tonight, I'm not working but it's tricky with us

Once I greet all four directions
I am left unbuttoned by the exits
you wait for me, virtual and high
and I yeah yeah yeah until you
find your conjured shape